My Name Is Mudd

ISBN – 13: 978-1463742386
ISBN – 10: 146374238X

All rights reserved © 2011 Southpaw Books. First Printing: 2011. The editorial arrangement, analysis and professional commentary are subject to this copyright notice. No portion of this book may be copied, retransmitted, reposted, duplicated or otherwise used without the express written approval of the author, except by reviewers who may quote brief excerpts in connection with a review.

United States laws and regulations are public domain and not subject to copyright. Any unauthorized copying, reproduction, translation or distribution of any part of this material without permission by the author is prohibited and against the law.

Disclaimer and Terms of Use: Southpaw Books assumes no liability or responsibility for damage or injury to you, other persons or property arising from any use of any product, information, idea or instruction contained in the content or services provided to you through this book. Reliance upon information contained in this material is solely at the reader's own risk. The author has no financial interest in and receives no compensation from manufacturers of products or websites mentioned in this book.

My Name is Mudd

Facebook Posts and other (A)musings

Jeff Mudd

For Jennifer, McKenzie,
McCoy and Mitchell.

In loving memory of my pop,
Joe Mudd

Foreward

I post; therefore I am…

… planning to get the kids a Christmas gift that keeps on giving the whole year through — a paper route.

…getting so old that I have a few blue chest hairs.

…wishing my wife would look at me the way she does her shoes.

…wondering if an obese person goes swimming if it's still considered skinny dipping?

…thinking that the new mystery novel by weatherman Al Roker has a 90% chance of sucking.

Since joining Facebook in 2009 and reacquainting with friends both past and present, I have been tossing such tidbits on my wall. I have some 400 pals (some of whom I can't quite place, and vice versa), and I would love to have them all over two weeks from Tuesday for coffee and bundt cake. But that would be against my HOA regulations. Instead, I try to add a dash of spice to the daily grind. Some posts stick; others don't, as the laws of humor (and pasta) dictate. Not everyone can be made to laugh. Such is the fate of the funny.

Facebook in itself is an odd place. Lots of people to see, stuff to do, hours to waste. It has replaced soap operas and game shows as the daytime time suck. Mark Zuckerberg is the new Bob Barker, our resident Bo Brady. But I don't poke or politic or tomcat or tag, nor do I hold any affiliation to the make-believe Mafia or reside on a fictional farm. I rarely share vacation photos of places you haven't been or highlight snapshots of food that you wish you were eating.

I don't begrudge those who do. A plate of meat and a family in Crete both deserve their due. It's just that my Facebook nook has always been to try and add some levity to the everyday. Many of the posts focus on love and marriage and family, others on pop culture/sports and current events and holidays. Health (by day, I'm a fitness trainer) and beauty (by night, I live in suburban Austin) also both make appearances. Just Seinfeldian, routine stuff, and everyone and everything are fair game. To be sure, celebrities are roasted, but, in fairness, so is my family and, especially, myself. I also pepper in some jabs at the world and its many wonderful warts, delivered in a cynical manner that is decidedly deadpan.

I never intended to do anything with these swings at humor, other than to perhaps, well, humor. But there are some 129 million books in print, including a novel by renowned scribe Hillary Duff, a book of poetry from noted philosopher Keanu Reeves and a puzzling number of books on the subject of dirt. Just. Plain. Dirt. Surely, I thought, there's room for one about just plain Mudd. Just to cover myself, though, I also chose a smaller book size that can double nicely as a coaster for your highball.

There's a sign in my place of business that reads "Live, Love, Laughter." I always keep it turned over so that the well-worn slogan is reversed. To me, the world, too often ridiculous in the worst of ways, is to be laughed at and often flipped on its head.

Herein, I rarely post about the many things about my family – my wife Jennifer, daughter McKenzie and sons McCoy and Mitchell – that make me proud. I could write an entire book, or at least a large pamphlet, about such moments. And in each chapter introduction, I even steer from sarcasm for the sake of letting them know, as they say, how I really feel.

In large part, though, the following is written with tongue planted firmly in cheek. It is my Hallmark card to them and to the world, only it's located at Spencer's Gifts, next to the bag of farts and the Lamborghini mirror.

Baby

I speak to him, and he briefly looks my way, then away. I am nothing, a stranger, a whisper in the dark. This baby, it occurs to me, doesn't yet understand that his mom isn't the only boob in the house.

I am hovering above Mitchell, and he couldn't care less. He is just eight weeks old now and still has a trace of that wonderful new-baby smell. He is shifty and fat and lazy and needy. Essentially, he is my Uncle Stu in a onesey. I couldn't love him more if I tried. Mitchell, not Stu.

To report that the kid was an outright surprise would be inaccurate. With already two in tow, the wife and I were pretty sure how to cook one up – and how to avoid such. But after a couple of years of misfires and misadventures, we were pretty sure, the way you sometimes just sense, that our family was destined to be a foursome. This was fine. This was our family album.

It's said that watched pots never boil, and a year later our incidental, accidental miracle arrived. Mitch was bigger than the two before him, tipping the scales at nine-plus pounds, and is just now mastering a big, toothy, goofy smile. He is happy and hungry, and his eyes are wide with wonder. As with all my children during their infancies, I just can't stop looking at him. I stare with amazement. With gratitude. And, sometimes, with envy. His entire story lies before him. His biggest concerns, like that of Uncle Stu, are gas and bloating. He is a miniature life in waiting, an empty cup. My wish is that he fills his life to the brim.

Parents in the know (and oddly, people who have no children at all) like to joke that three kids are one too many, that the man-to-man defense must be switched to a zone. And in these matters, it is true: three is to two as the population of Texas is to, say, Delaware. But to me, five feels right. Five fingers. Five toes. Five Mudds.

We are whole. We are one.

Got a McCoy and a McKenzie. This stick tells us to start soliciting McNames for a new McMudd. Early frontrunner: McJagger.

Doc said that the baby should be beginning his descent. I asked her if we should put our tray tables up and turn off our cell phones. She wrote something down.

Readying for the hospital, it occurred to me that I was wearing the same shirt as the day my 9-year-old daughter was born. This speaks volumes for my memory and absolutely nothing for my wardrobe.

New kid weighed in at 9-plus pounds. They rolled him right past the nursery and over to Ed's Big & Tall Shop.

The drive home from the hospital with a new baby is always an extra-safe ride. An Amish couple just trotted by and flipped us off.

He's slow and chunky and can hold a squat for hours. Heading to Academy Sports to get the baby a catcher's mitt.

This new kid is cute as can be. Not much for eye contact, though. Gotta work on that before his first job interview.

There's no denying that most babies, regardless of race, religion or gender, look a lot like Buddy Hackett on a bender.

Enjoy your first day at home, sweet boy. There's a stack of newspapers to fold at 4 a.m.

I stared deeply into the eyes of my newborn son, awestruck by just how much joy the human heart can hold, and he peed on my face.

Baby's probable first words: "Dude, you gotta stop staring at me. It's really freaking me out."

With a first child, a dropped pacifier is cause for a thorough sterilization; with the second, the five-second rule is in effect; this third kid just needs to understand that pacifiers come with carpet fuzz and other shrapnel.

Toss-up as to what's more complex – unraveling a terrorist plot, splitting an atom or correctly buttoning this onesey.

Relearning the slow, stiff-legged walk employed while nearing the crib with a sleeping baby. Perfected by parents. And zombies.

Well, I guess this little guy is going to stick around. Back to the bottom of the totem pole for me.

Work

Burning is good, unless it's during urination.

Such has been my mantra these past 11 years in the exercise field. Combine lactic acid with laughter. Originally a sportswriter and would-be novelist, the spark for my life swap ignited from simple observation and deduction. In other words, I watched some pot-bellied schmucks making a buck at it and figured that I could do it, too.

It's a good enough living, provided one doesn't need to reside in a high-rise penthouse. Admittedly, my career ladder has always been something of a stepstool. That's fine; I know what money can do to people. I've seen "Behind the Music" on VH-1.

Besides, I never grew up with childhood fantasies (Heather Locklear notwithstanding) or felt a calling to be the president or a vet or a male stripper. I simply wanted to do something that I enjoyed and to stay out of a hair net or a clip-on tie. Anything in between, provided it provided, would be fine.

So the workout bit came to be, and it's been a fun run. I suppose I make a big impression on the lives of a select few, leave a dent on others and cause hardly a scratch on the rest. Essentially, I'm a Wal-Mart greeter dressed like Chachi. Maybe I make your day; maybe I don't.

Training is akin to writing in that most anyone can do it, yet not many can do it well, and fewer still well enough to put food on the table. I've been fortunate to find work that doesn't much feel like work. Like any job, the gig turns to grind on occasion, but it beats coal mining, and I'm in a profession in which I have the right to bare arms. Sure, most people would prefer to pop a pill and, voila, have a Photoshopped figure, but until there's an app for that, I'll likely have a job.

Along with the obvious tricks of the trade – pulling clients in and then pushing them to push themselves, not always an innate skill – an effective trainer also must be a good listener, a loyal confidant and, often, a shrink in Spandex. Father Flanagan doesn't know as many secrets as we do. Over an hour's time, we may weave words with weights, counsel while we count and listen as we lift. So if you have a trainer and he appears confused, assume that he is just thinking really, really hard.

For me, the training world is somewhat of a nine-to-five mirage. Inside the walls of a gym, women listen attentively to what I have to say, trust my judgement, carry out my instructions and, at month's end, hand me a check. I am somebody. Away from the gym, of course, none of the above applies. I am nobody.

We trainers battle against the latest and greatest. The Four-Minute Beach Body Workouts as shown by the genetically perfect fitness model. The Killer Abs in 2.66 Easy Moves by the bulimic reality-television star. The Thighmasters and Gazelles and vibrating belts of the world. The fads and fasts and props and potions and Shake Weights and miracle shakes. The short cuts. At times some of our flock even wanders off in pursuit of the quick fix; they often wander (or waddle) back for the long haul. No pain. No gain. No exceptions.

People enlist trainers for different means, but most want the same rewards in the end. To live longer. To live stronger. And by that I mean: to look better naked. Some people are willing to sacrifice; others are not. Many could manage on their own; others wouldn't know (or care) the difference between an upright row and a Hibachi Grill. A few put in the extra work; many clock out upon leaving the gym.

The body doesn't really speculate about the motives. It only cares about the facts, and you can't fake out the facts. Work hard. Eat right. Get sleep. Drink water. Be consistent. Rinse and repeat. Even with all that, one's genes usually play the most pivotal role in the size jeans one wears.

This is the truth.

And the truth, like the shorts of Richard Simmons, never really changes.

An hour of exercise purportedly adds seven minutes to one's life. No idea if they will be quality minutes. You could easily be drinking Salisbury steak through a straw or clapping mindlessly like Paula Abdul.

The salary of my first job out of college was 14K, and that was back when 14K wasn't a lot of money.

It's never too late to start exercising. My friend's granny, for instance, didn't take up walking until she was 92. They don't know where the hell she is.

Working out while listening to Meatloaf. Ironic.

Saw the Chicken Tenders Basket here has 77 grams of fat, thus ending my tenders affair with chicken baskets.

To keep things in perspective, I denounce Fat Tuesday in lieu of Big-Boned Tuesday or Muscle-Weighs-More-Than-Fat Tuesday.

Tweaked my back bending over to pick up my reading glasses; I want to be your fitness professional.

I believe my clients like me but hate my workouts. I'm okay with this. Their affection brings them in, and their disdain pays my mortgage.

As I gaze proudly at my new vacuum cleaner (sleek! cordless!), much as a proud father does a newborn child, I realize that I've owned my gym much too long.

Trying to bring back terry cloth headbands and wristbands. I'm truly committed to this. Please, help me in my endeavors.

I buff the women; the husbands get the spoils. I am nothing but a fluffer.

Today, in honor of Jack Lalane's passing, my clients will do only pushups, sit-ups, jumping jacks and tractor pulls with their teeth.

Taking the week off from the gym to give my clients a chance to slip into the Fitness Protection Program.

It takes 17 muscles to smile and 47 to frown but, for the sake of energy conservation, only a couple to stare off blankly into space.

The road to hell is paved with unused workout clothes jammed in the side pocket of a suitcase.

Learned early in my training career to be wary of female clients wearing a matching outfit, a full complement of makeup and Charlie perfume.

One constant and absolute truth I've found after a decade in the fitness industry is this: Women always look better than they think, and men never look as good as they think.

My first real job was as a sportswriter. My folks enjoyed reading my stuff. More than that, they enjoyed having written proof that I had a job.

On a few occasions during a decade of gym ownership, I've considered torching this place for insurance purposes. The simple truth of the matter, though, is that chrome just doesn't burn well.

My clients get spooked by pops and cracks in their joints. I tell them that pops are only small gaseous explosions, similar to the ones they often let fly while doing sit-ups.

Woke to find I'd been inducted into the National Association of Professional Women Trainers. This was obviously a mistake. I'm not that professional.

"Sorry, I just had a client go down on me." This was the wrong explanation to give the wife when asked about my tardiness due to a client fainting.

Pretty good weight loss idea – spend a couple of days at Sea World in August. I weighed 67 pounds this morning.

If a female client gets a haircut, I ask her if she's lost weight. If she gets new shoes, I ask her if she's lost weight. I am learning.

Not feeling it at work today. I introduced myself as an Impersonal Trainer.

New client told me she'd Googled me a while back then forgot about it; not the first time a woman has been unimpressed with my Google.

Okay, so all I need to start my own P90Xian Empire is a dimly lit room, a few muscle-bound sidekicks, a techno CD and several hundred thousand start-up dollars?

Sometimes I wish that clients fought for the last few reps like they'll fight for control of the remote.

Richard Simmons inspires me to be a kinder man, a more motivating trainer, and a heterosexual.

No matter how many times I ask women to do ball twists, it just never rolls off the tongue.

What, you mean you worked out twice last month, ate poorly, did only enough cardio to remain clinically alive and didn't lose any weight? Ma'am, with all due respect, I'm a personal trainer, not the Lord Almighty

McCoy

A father's dreams for his son are simple and pure. Let him be healthy and happy. Let him spread laughter and joy. Let him find friendship and love. Let him be a good husband, father and friend. Let him prosper in life.

And by all that I mean, please let him one day sign a lucrative, multi-year contract to be the next great shortstop for the Yankees.

My best buddy is four years old. McCoy is full of fire and brimstone, with wild blonde hair and, at times, an even wilder streak. His sippy cup runneth over with affection, but sometimes, over the course of a weekend, he drives me insane. Not figuratively, clinically. In the same breath, I am crazy about him. There is no human being that I have ever felt closer to. It can be a job with no overtime benefits, the maintaining of McCoy, but I just can't quit him.

We're just getting started on the Andy-and-Opie thing. We don't hunt or fish or change the oil together, and possibly never will, because I really don't know how to do any of that. But one day I will have a catch with him and will show him how to shave. I will warn him about fast females and will preach to him about slow driving. I will try to teach him what I've learned, often the hard way, as I, in turn, learn from him. More and more, I find that much of what I know I learned not in, but because of, a kindergartener.

That is for another day. Right now, our chief pastime consists of just hanging out. We laugh and bicker and play and barter. We make forts and take walks and fake wrestle and watch cartoons. There are periods of bartering and litigation littered with good times and bad times and Polaroid moments and head-in-hands moments. We are best friends, and even though we don't always understand what the other is saying, we'll figure out the exact parameters of that friendship as we go along.

I know it won't always be this way, our peas-and-carrots bit, and that he won't always lean on me as he does today. His buddies and pursuits and libido will inevitably trump his graying old man. At times, as I watch him, I get glimpses of the man he might become, but they are still hazy, without borders. Will he, I wonder, obediently fall into line on the conveyor belt of life? Or will he swim against the status quo? Will he shrug off failure and stand up to adversity? Will he accept that the world is a casserole of good and bad, ups and downs, wins and losses? Will he look after his little brother as mine (Jay, Mike and Steve) have looked after me? Will he learn, in due time, to be wary of a woman who carries too many bags and has too much baggage?

And will he one day lay in bed, as I often do, and wonder and worry the very same about his own son?

Above all else, I hope that he clings to the core sweetness that is his hallmark. Even today, in his own Rosetta Stone way, he reminded me, out of the blue, that he "wuved me" 40-42 times and hugged me half as many. With McCoy, you always know exactly where you stand. In a world of transparent smiles and hidden agendas, how many people in our lives can we say that about?

One day, after he graduates from Dr. Seuss U. and ends his torrid affair with Dora the Explorer, he will read this. It is likely to embarrass him, perhaps even anger him. It is then that I will slowly slide my arm around his shoulder, give him a loving squeeze and remind him of the time he pantsed me in Starbucks when he was three.

Paybacks, kid, paybacks.

Statistically, the odds of McCoy ever playing in the major leagues are thin. For scoring a fat contract with the Yankees, slimmer still. As for scoring with Minka Kelly, well…the kid has curly blonde hair, blue eyes and a golden heart. Hey, it's baseball; it ain't over 'til it's over.

This kid asks 'why' more than Nancy Kerrigan.

The boy's first soccer practice was probably much like the SXSW Music Festival — organized chaos, multiple drink breaks, everybody looking to score…

The boy is really picking up soccer, and by that I mean picking up the ball and running with it.

Saw the fish sticks I served the boy are made from minced fish. I can't wait to one day wake him up early, walk together down to the crick and take him fishing for mince.

Slugger Barry Bonds and the boy have something in common; before going to baseball practice, they both need some juice.

This kid has the bladder control of Mickey Rooney.

Maybe the boy wasn't the biggest or the fastest or the strongest on the playground, but he easily had the best hair, so he's still going to win.

The boy is a firm director with a precise vision of how things should be. He is Marty Scorsese, with better hair, or Woody Allen, but taller.

I sometimes stare at the boy, my handsome son, and miss our old mailman.

The boy was wearing high heels, and mismatched ones at that, when I picked him up at Sunday School, proving religion can indeed be transformational.

Thanks to his big sister, this boy will be ready and waiting for the torturous ways of women.

Boy going in to get tubes in his ears; I asked the doctor if, while he was at it, he could surgically stuff plugs in mine.

Each time my son gives me his flying knee drop, the scientific odds of him ever having a younger sibling decrease by millions.

Santa Claus brought the boy a Slinkee. He enjoyed the hell out of it for three minutes, until it was snarled and in the trash.

The boy has mastered the three most important words to know when dealing with a door-to-door salesman – "Beat it, weasel." – and seems eager to try it out on the next unsuspecting Girl Scout.

He won't say so, but I can always tell when this kid needs to drop a deuce by his Elephant Man walk

The boy tells it like it is. He got a warm-up suit today for Christmas. Me: "Hey kid, you know what you do with a warm-up suit? He: "Warm up."

Trying to teach the kid to use his 37 pounds as leverage for the safe and proper operation of the weed whacker.

The boy got bit on the hand at daycare today. While I was comforting him, his teacher said, "Well, he kicked at me today, so he didn't have a very good day, either." I told her that nobody likes a tattle tale.

While admittedly biased, I believe this kid owns the best blonde 'fro since Ian Zehring.

The boy's annunciation of "chocolate" is shorter and sounds way too much like a male reproductive organ; hence, it was a little uncomfortable when he said, loudly, that he wanted some in a crowded restaurant.

The only thing slower than my crawl out of the kid's bed after finally getting him to sleep is erosion.

Dialogue on the way to church: Boy: "Daddy, why we go to church?" Me: "Because there's someone way up in the sky that gives us all the good things we have, and we need to go say thank you." Boy: "Santa Claus?"

If this kid asked for a Porsche in exchange for having a good day at preschool, I would readily promise it to him. Of course, I wouldn't buy him a Porsche. He's three; he doesn't know what he wants.

Made some freezer pops with the boy. Reminded me of when I was a little tot. Also reminded me that freezer pops aren't that great.

Watching a show about a kid genius while my son picks cheese doodles out of his eyebrows.

Just met (UT quarterback) Colt McCoy while with my son, McCoy, who was wearing his Colt McCoy jersey. Colt looked a little freaked out until I introduced our daughter, Earl Campbell.

Life

To borrow some words from 'ol Brooks, the crusty librarian from "The Shawshank Redemption:"

"The world went and got in a big damn hurry."

Reportedly, we are flooded with some 1,500 advertising messages each day (fewer for the Amish). Supposedly, we human types have about 3,000 thoughts per day (or roughly the accumulative number for the cast of "Jersey Shore"). And somehow, between rise and sleep, we find time to spit out approximately 13,500 words (20,000 for females; 7,000 for males; 13,500 for Penn; 0 for Teller).

I challenge you to keep your eyes open. To keep your thoughts original. To make your words fresh.

Things happen in the world and in our lives that beg for some levity. In our home, we call the first 20-odd minutes of the nightly news the "bad news." Accounts of human tragedies and natural disasters are sandwiched around the occasional fluff piece about a man who grew a strawberry t resembles, say, Kelly Ripa. It's all enough to dull even the brightest of optimists. Besides, I think you'll agree that Kelly Ripa is a peach, not a strawberry.

    Admittedly, I'm as guilty as anyone of drifting into Doomsday thinking (the wife will second this). Know how people never think 'it' will happen to them? I'm always shocked when it *doesn't* happen to me. My life is a Rapture yet to happen, and, as for that Floridian-shaped mole on my shoulder, don't even get me and Web MD started. But in terms of the everyday, I can milk humor out of the driest of subjects. Not on another man's or region's misfortune, certainly, but on the simple magic of the mundane.

    I believe the repetitious hum of life too often lulls our brains into auto pilot. We are force fed information and, without chewing on it or swishing it around, quickly digest it as the humdrum gospel. Make light of the drab. Once in a while, be a sculptor of sarcasm. Twist your words into a balloon animal.

    Things can get heavy. Think light.

As 80,000 motorcyclists converge for the Republic of Texas Rally, Austin becomes, for one glorious weekend at least, the Back Hair Capital of the World.

Saw you can purchase an authentic bottle of Texas Rain at the drugstore here. If you get lost, it's right next to the Cans of Sun and Tubes of Wind.

As a transplanted Austinite, I sometimes feel like I should get in touch with my inner hippy, but I've tried, and he's pretty gamey.

Double sinus infection; not as awesome as a double rainbow.

When I hear my late father's voice that's still on my mom's voice mail, it makes me sad and happy and nostalgic and sometimes hopeful that he's just screening my call because I need money.

We Texans struggle a bit with the cold. Several here at the coffeehouse weeping openly, a man using a bagel as earmuffs, a woman sawing off her leg for provisions…

Just counted out 42 consecutive sneezes, shattering both my own Southwest regional record and your belief that I don't have exciting Friday night plans.

I'm old enough to remember when being a viral sensation wasn't really a good thing.

Couldn't endorse the married couple sitting in church today wearing Pittsburgh Steelers jerseys: (1) because they were wearing jerseys in church and (2) if God is a football fan, He would certainly back the poor and meek and defenseless, like the Browns.

It's impossible to look like anything except a tool when riding a Ferris Wheel.

Just got a notice from a small-town Justice of the Peace regarding an unpaid speeding ticket issued in November of 1993, thus satisfying that pesky stack of to-do's on the desk of Mabel the City Secretary.

If they're called leaves, then why am I always picking them up?

My peanut butter crackers are made with *real* peanut butter, which is both comforting to me and heroic of them.

The many emails I receive each day regarding male enhancement products, some addressed directly to me, give me ego shrinkage.

Not sure why folks in joints that sell local coffees and sprouts and such are often so contemplative, unsure and timid when ordering. The only logical conclusion I can come up with is that, with the obvious exception of the naturally contemplative, unsure and timid, they are really, really high.

Saw the oldest inmate on Texas death row died before his execution. Cause of death — suspense.

Experiencing waves of anxiety, fear and panic, along with feelings of desperation, isolation and ignorance here in the tools aisle at Home Depot.

Love it when I leave church feeling like my heart needs Spanx.

When somebody at a party half-heartedly asks you what you do (for a living), answer with the obvious: "About what?"

Had to answer four questions to obtain a small coffee from the synthetically perky barista, or two more than I would have to answer to legally buy a gun to shoot her.

The average book sells 173 copies — most to family and friends — so I'm determined to either (1) write a better-than-average book or (2) find more family and friends.

Read that the world's most literate country is Iceland, where I guess brain freezes don't apply.

Life Certainty #1 – If a co-worker is out sick, even with the most obscure of ailments, say, rickets, another co-worker will walk by and knowingly tell you that "Yeah, that's really going around."

Life Certainty #2 – If it is raining, even if you live in Seattle or the Amazon Rainforest, somebody will breeze past and knowingly tell you that "Boy, we really needed it."

Life Certainty #3: When a reality show contestant is voted off the show and emphatically promises viewers that "you haven't seen the last of me," it will be the last you see of him.

Five razor blades for 13 bucks leave me wondering if ZZ Top needs a roadie.

Think I accidentally took the dog's anti-inflammatory pill and gave the dog my multi-vitamin, as evidenced by the fact that my hips haven't felt this good in years, and that my dog just dropped a blue deuce.

To contact me, you need not "fire me off an email" or "rattle my cage" or "buzz my tower" or "shoot me a text." Just give me a call.

Heading to the hardware store to do something I thought I'd never do — buy a hoe.

Saw the French restaurant near the gym closed down, leaving me scrambling for a place to get a really bad French lunch for $14.94.

There's been so much foreplay surrounding the BCS Championship Game (between Texas and Alabama) that I suspect most men won't last three minutes into it.

Is still yet to see an anvil that wasn't made out of cartoons.

"At the end of the day" inches past "it is what it is" as the world's most obvious and overused cliché. Really. Seriously.

Watching Penn State v. Wisconsin. Can't be sure, but I'd bet that Penn State Coach Joe Paterno, earphones in place on the sidelines,
has instead been listening to Paul Anka for years.

ect an entire theme song by Kenny
ut it would be kinda nice if my life were

backed by the music of an up-and-coming singer/songwriter, like the last 18 minutes of every "Grey's Anatomy."

Just got back from Mexico. I miss it already. Everybody there called me Jefe, or "boss."

No offense to Austin meteorologists, but for roughly 10.8 months out of the year, they could likely replace themselves with cardboard cutouts and insert an audio loop, and nobody would be the wiser.

Heard a guy brag that he's a better lover than most men because he's never "pleasured himself." I say he's just lazy.

So I have a battery charger for my phone and Ipod and camera and razor and weed eater. Where's one for my battery?

Brainwashed from too many cartoons as a child, I actually walked around a banana peel today for fear of slipping.

Back on the golf course after a year of self-imposed retirement. I should have never come back here to work.

Trying to golf with thin irons called blades. I think I'll just fall on mine.

I have no problem with the fleet of Austinites who use bicycles as their primary mode of transportation. I wonder, however, if they would mind my driving 35 MPH on the sidewalk while they pedal 3 MPH in the middle of the lane?

Note to dads – be careful not to end a text to a teenage babysitter with a ;) instead of a :).

If reaching the pinnacle of success means affixing one of those PermaPhones into my ear, the ones that remind me of the torture roaches implanted in the dude's brain in "Star Trek II: The Wrath of Khan," then you can have it.

I sometimes rise in the morning, take a good, long look at myself in the mirror, and feel the need to be Photoshopped.

Overbearing soccer coach/frustrated ex-jock on the playground. I give him 2-3 weeks in the league, and 42-45 years on the Earth.

Read that flossing increases life expectancy, then made an appointment with an estate planner.

Sure, I'm 41 years old, but, thanks to a series of elixirs and ointments and late-night infomercial steals, I don't feel a day older than 47.

I share a birthday with John Ritter, which makes sense, and Flo Rida, which doesn't.

Am driving a house en route to camping with 30 people and henceforth only answering to the name Jim Jones.

At the campsite. Over the next 72 hours, we'll be reminded, time and again, that Mudds simply don't camp.

The term 'porn star' is overused. Very few of them are stars. I tend to think of most of them as (highly questionable) character actors.

In America, more Frisbees are sold annually than all the basketballs, baseballs, volleyball, tennis balls and footballs combined. Righteous.

Drinking Fat Tire beer could give one a Spare Tire where once there was a Flat Tire.

Love going to the car wash. Drive out feeling like I have just purged my (con)sole.

Round Rock ISD test scores markedly higher than those in Austin ISD. In other words, boss me around while you still can, because one day my kids are going to need your kids to, uh, yeahhh, come in for work on Saturday.

Guys never get invited to any of these trunk show exchanges that women are always hosting, probably because there's no such thing as an article of clothing that a guy thinks he doesn't need anymore.

Got nabbed by the nice-but-talkative next-door neighbor while doing yard work. Could he not see that I was raking fake leaves?

3:52 a.m. – I'm too heavy of a thinker to be such a light sleeper.

Someday, the college kid that I just asked to read my credit card's expiration date to me will in turn ask another college kid to read her card's expiration date for her.

When solicited by a political campaign pollster, just quickly mention that you're a convicted felon. The call will be brief.

The guy frantically waving his cell phone in the air to try and make a text go through is the same guy who pushes the elevator 'up' button 17 times.

I fully intend to pass along to my kids the true meaning of life, as soon as someone passes it along to me.

Journalists who write 'spoiler alert!' just before writing the spoiler understand very little about human nature.

Just got an official-sounding call from Manilow's people threatening a lawsuit for hairstyle infringement. Heading to the barber shop today.

It's my stance that the phrase Sexually Transmitted Disease should be changed back to Venereal Disease, which sounded much more menacing.

The music of "Explosions in the Sky" will make you want to reach for the stars.

Overheard a college coed having a conversation with a friend. Inside of two minutes, she said "like" 42 times. I'm not too sure I like her chances in, like, the world.

Dog parks, with all their posturing and sniffing and crap, make me appreciate marriage.

Just mowed the yard. Texas summers are brutal. Even my sweat was sweating.

I worry about sushi fanatics, whose vocal passion of raw fish borders on the orgasmic and leaves me wondering if everything else in their lives is anticlimactic.

If life gives you lemons, make lemonade.
If it gives you beets, throw that crap away. Those things are nasty.

Well of course I want to hear, at length, about the playoff prospects of your fantasy football team. When you're done, would you mind checking out this cyst while watching the slideshow of our family vacation to Detroit?

I'm too old for many of life's pleasures but evidently still young enough for zits.

Had to put down our 13-year-old dog Jack, a good friend and loyal pet. Getting him cremated and will place his remains on the mantel – our Jack in the Box.

Missing Jack but must admit that he is now much easier to take for a walk.

Big loser in poker last night. The new guy had 'hustler' written all over him; this was in contrast to regular player Todd, who has "subscribes to Hustler" written all over him.

Next to our favorite Italian food restaurant, there is a store that specializes in VCR Cleaning. Business is slow.

Have never actually heard an old-timer say that he "walked three miles to school, uphill, in the snow, barefoot...," but if I did, I would probably consider him to be either suffering from early-stage dementia or to be an outright liar.

This dude in front of me in line would need a court order to get his hair to move.

Dated a beauty queen after college, but it didn't last long. We really only had one thing in common – I was in love with her, and she was in love with her, too.

It's been my experience that people who use the phrase "that's what's wrong with America" are often people who are wrong with America.

Life is a Fuddrucker's. We all get a slab of meat. Make of it what you will.

McKenzie

As I watched her being hoisted above the curtain in the delivery room, I still wasn't sure that I was ready for my daughter. First-time parenthood, even at 32, can be something of a heavy concept, an anvil on the head of independence.

Today, I'm comforted to know that nobody is ever completely ready for my daughter.

McKenzie doesn't actually enter a room as much as she plays it. There isn't a full-length mirror not worthy of a double take, or a sequined costume that shouldn't be tried on, or an animated conversation that isn't worth having. She is a mayor, an emcee, a game-show host. There's a shy side there, but it's buried deep under a feathered boa and trampled by Go-Go boots and muted by a snappy Broadway tune.

She has been making us laugh for years and fires off "postworthy" one-liners all the time. (I don't often chronicle them. See: Plate, Meat.) With her funny faces and choreographed crashes, she reminds me of a young John Ritter in pigtails, right down to the patented couch flip. Sure, she is prone to apocalyptic drama and overacting along the lines of Matthew McConaughey, and, because of such, she may receive some glazed-over stares along her path. She will need to grow accustomed to the "smuckle," which is the lovechild of the smirk and the chuckle. I know it well. She's a sandwich of sorts, our first-born child. Usually a ham, sometimes cheesey, always wry.

It may trouble, say, a Rhodes Scholar, but I'm proud to see that she shares my philosophy that life can always be improved with a splash of humor. You can't always be the smartest person in the room, or the most successful, or the most glamorous, but you can at least make fun of their haircuts.

I got a preview of what might lie ahead when she was four or so. I was driving the two of us home, and she stumbled across a piece of candy in the backseat. This exchange followed:

She – "Hey daddy, can I have this piece of chocolate?"
Me – "No babe, we're about to eat. After dinner, okay?"

Silence. Then the ruffling of papers. Then me glimpsing into the rear-view mirror to see her chocolate-covered face.
Me – "McKenzie? Did you just eat that candy right after I told you not to?"
Silence.
Me – "McKenzie!"
Pause.
She – "Hey daddy….I really like your shirt."

She's 10 now and gets more pretty and outgoing by the day. While I wish her no ill will – no acne scars or broken hearts – I sometimes pray for a five-year bout with chronic halitosis (ages 13-18). Is that so wrong? I concede that I will soon be a distant housemate, a public embarrassment and a no-interest banker. Piggyback rides will give way to a new car; braces will bow to beauty; Barbies will take – go ahead and shoot me now – a backseat to boys. I will watch her grow and mature and laugh and love, but too often only from the cheap seats of her life.

It is during this period when she will keep me at arm's length that I hope she keeps her wit, and her wits about her. That she remains a character while holding on to her character. She is silly but strong, McKenzie, and she'll need to be. See, there is a boy out there right now. His name is likely Preston or Austin or Miles, and one day he will pull into our driveway in a fast car with questionable intentions for my little girl.

I may not have been quite ready for her, but I hope McKenzie will be ready for this punk Preston.

At the beach. 12:15p-3:12p: Me: "Please just get in the ocean, McKenzie, I *promise* the jellyfish won't get you." 3:13p: McKenzie in ocean. 3:16p: McKenzie at lifeguard stand being treated for a jellyfish sting.

Stopped at a truck-stop bathroom on a road trip. Thought it best to bring the girl into the men's room with me. She: "So dad, what's a Rough Rider condom with raised rubber ridges?" Me: "Kid, if I knew, you wouldn't be here."

The girl broke wind. While doing so, she put her hand behind her. Me: "What was that?" She: "Heh-heh, my fart silencer."

The daughter bemoaned forgetting her video-game thing on the way to the movies, sentencing her to 4-6 minutes of original thought.

The girl won a red ribbon in her first gymnastics meet. It would have been a blue if it weren't for the damn Ukranian judge.

The girl has a friend over. Overheard from downstairs: Friend: "Oh, sorry, my mom doesn't let me watch PG-13 movies." McKenzie: "So just don't tell her?" Oh crap.

There are few things in life as dramatic as when the girl has to swallow a pill — a Lifetime movie, a Rose Ceremony, a very special episode of Blossom...

The girl is having fun at camp. She reported that her first day was filled with lots of "I dunno, stuff." This, of course, differs from the "I dunno, stuff" she does at her friends' houses, and the "I dunno, stuff" she learns at school.

Kudos to the girl, who has made it to her ninth year without the benefit of vegetables or floss.

In a lottery to get the girl tickets to the Miley Cyrus concert. I would probably have to go along to, you know, chaperone. Fingers crossed for, um, her.

The girl has developed the ability to transition without effort from an angel to the antichrist and back; she's becoming a woman.

Still carrying the girl (9) up to bed at night.
Not sure which will go first — my back, or her off to college.

Carried the sleep-talking daughter up to bed. She whispered, "Oranges. Trees are good. Patriots go." Heavy, kid, heavy.

The girl goes through four, five costume changes a day; we're raising Cher.

One day I will preach to the girl that nothing good happens after midnight, when boys turn into nocturnal jerks.

The girl is bummed. No ice on the road, so no school cancellation. She foresaw it, though, by predicting there wasn't going to be enough "anticipation" to freeze over.

It's a tough day when your daughter becomes old enough to call you out on your BS.

Got some food at McDonald's. The girl says, "Dad, I want to work at McDonald's." I say, "Yeah? That's not a bad high-school job." She says, "No, I mean when I grow up." Reach for the stars, kid.

At the girl's dance recital. For the love of good God, it's longer than Beowulf.

At the skating rink with the girl, keeping a close eye on the balding guy in skinny jeans while nursing the blood blister I got from getting the fourth-highest score in Centipede.

The girl is starting to have epic phone conversations with friends. I tell her she's going to get cauliflower ear. She rolls her eyes and walks away. Yeah, it didn't work on me, either.

Armed with binoculars and a wireless mike, dressed in camouflage, stashed away in a bush, I am feeding the girl answers to a TAKS passage titled "Joseph Glidden: Father of Barbed Wire."

My daughter greets each day by watching a rerun of "Full House," forcing me to reluctantly rerun my man crush on Uncle Jessie and to rehash a time when I was confused.

The girl is wearing something that loosely resembles a bra; thankfully, she doesn't have anything that remotely resembles a breast.

The girl emerged from her first sleepover camp impressed not with the boys but with the size of the cinnamon rolls. And this is a very good thing.

At her second sleepover camp, the girl called to say that she had danced with "about 24" boys. And this is a very bad thing.

Me: "24 boys?!?" She: "Well, I can't tell them no dad!" Kid, for the love of all that is good and holy, learn.

Holidays

I am a Grinch. Each Christmas Eve, I warn the kids that Santa Claus, with his weight problems and poor diet, is a prime candidate for heart attack, high blood pressure, stroke and even diabetes. He may show; he may not.

Truth be told, I'm still not over SantaGate, 1977. I went snooping through my mom's closet and, behind one of her pantsuits, found a Green Monster, which was the sequel to the Stretch Armstrong (if you are male, you are nodding your head in remembrance). So, expecting to unwrap my new amphibious friend on Christmas morning, he was instead propped in the "Santa Stack," all scaley and stretchy and ready to, in due time, be dissected and drained of his super-powered corn syrup.

Thus, I spent my ninth Christmas tugging, half-heartedly, on my Green Monster.

I submit now, with some exceptions, that we Americans feel the need to honor occasions more occasionally than we really need to. I train some state and federal officials, and I'm always surprised when they're *not* off for a holiday. MLK certainly deserves a nod, but a tree? Baby Jesus is worthy, but Christopher Columbus? Me, I decide to annually *not* honor a pillaging Italian rapist who accidentally discovered America. Veterans should indeed be saluted, but as for Labor Day, well, it's *labor* day. Why the free pass?

Let's be honest. In large part, holidays are for kids (Halloween, Christmas, etc.) and the shareholders of Hallmark (Valentine's Day, Father's and Mother's Day, etc.). As the years pass, so, too, does the excitement. Still, I try to squeeze the most out of them. On Halloween, I hand out inkless ballpoint pens and outdated magazines to eager trick-or-treaters. Nothing makes a 'Lil Goblin light up like a March, 2004 edition of Good Housekeeping. On New Year's Day, it's always fun to swear off my many vices, then see if my steely resolve outlasts the first half of the Chick-Fil-A Bowl. And on Valentine's Day, if the moon is right and the planets are aligned and the kids are sedated, I sometimes even get lucky.

Okay, so there is something to be said for the pageantry of holidays and, yes, it's nice to get together with extended family. Kids can brighten the bulb of most any day, never more than on a sleepy Christmas morning. Maybe I'm just still bitter over the self-inflicted wounds of 1977, when my imagination was stretched no more. Maybe I wasn't ready to not believe in magic. Maybe I didn't want to know, at age nine, that life is full of Green Monsters.

Happy Mother's Day. Without you, your kid would quite likely be dirty, hungry and wear stripes on plaid.

Easter was a day for renewal, redemption, and, for those of us intolerant to chocolate, reflux.

A whisker from getting busted here at home, the Easter Bunny escaped by a hare.

Coaching the boy on the techniques — the leg sweep, the injury fake, the flying elbow – that are imperative for Easter Egg Hunt victory.

I was broken up with, twice, on Valentine's Day. My wife can verify this because each February 14 I burn the photos of those women in effigy.
Then we go to Applebee's.

Arbor Day is not a big holiday around our house. We can either take it or leaf it.

Happy Good Friday, or as Mrs. Paul calls it, Christmas!

Saint Patrick converted thousands of pagans to Christianity and, most impressively, continues to keep Bennigan's in business.

Two clients in Cabo, one at the Grammys, another in Vegas, a fifth in Vail. Me, I went to Odessa for two days at Christmas.

The kids were just so-so this year, so I met them in the middle and in their stocking stuffed the greatest hits of Nat King Cole.

So long, Mr. Elf on the Shelf. For three weeks each year, your catatonic stare turns our children into upright, Elf-fearing citizens.

To scratch our philanthropic itch, we have decided to adopt a family for Xmas. I hope they don't mind all sleeping on the fold-out couch.

Am trying to tell the girl to embrace the coal that might fill her stocking, for in several million years she'll be dripping in diamonds.

Happy Father's Day to me. Today, I plan to put myself first. Until 8:42 a.m., when the kids will put me back in my place.

We considered looking for a kid friendly New Year's Eve event, but, honestly, our kids aren't overly friendly.

Happy Martin Luther King Day. Incidentally, I have a dream, too, only mine is recurring and includes wearing a unitard in the Quad.

Tomorrow is National Boss's Day.
Note to self — send wife flowers.

Ours are no longer with us, so in honor of Grandparents Day, we're headed to Luby's, where I will leave a $.72 tip.

To all veterans much braver than I and to those who didn't buy their camouflage at Old Navy, I salute you.

Happy Groundhog Day.
Happy Groundhog Day.
Happy Groundhog Day.

Kids

I am a liar. I am an extortionist and a con man. I am a kidnapper and a blackmailer and a broker of false hope.

I am a parent.

To survive, say, a 44-hour Saturday, one is likely to don one or more of these shady hats. We givers of care can only take so much, and there are times when we will do or give or say most anything and everything, whether it be truthful or not, in return for a millisecond of stop-action. We will cover honesty with them later; for now, we just need a flippin' minute.

For example, there was a recent Sunday when I was watching our trio solo, and, for kicks, I counted how many self-serving acts I committed over a three-hour span. I was pleasantly surprised to reach five; however, three of these involved the bathroom. (The can, incidentally, is sometimes the only sanctuary for a parent, assuming the kid didn't already break the lock. Call it Diplomatic Im-P.U.-nity.)

Out-of-body moments become commonplace in most every parent's life, scenes of humbling absurdity and temporary insanity that you didn't foresee when you were, say, a kid. When you were a nine-year-old with a head full of pipe dreams and a belly full of ice cream that was served to you, promptly, by your own parent. A young girl sees a sweet baby in her arms; she doesn't picture the projectile vomit. A little slugger envisions one day having a catch with his own son; he can't know that the kid will, at least initially, throw like a Nancy. Spilled drinks. Skinned knees. Spilled blood. Skinned feelings. Entertainment and arrangements to be provided, and *pronto*, with no Julie McCoy, your friendly cruise-ship director, in sight.

Nor do we fantasize that we will one day be cabbies and cooks and maids and butlers and tutors and, worse yet, virtually unnoticed for it all. Or hope that we, too, will quickly lick our fingers to tame a stray hair or count to one-two-threeee with menacing index fingers. And never, when we dreamed of being firemen or ballerinas or astronauts, did we imagine getting body slammed by six girls at a slumber party or spending $27 on a $1 stuffed something or dragging a screaming kid out of a store by the nostril. These things, these monstrosities, only happen to *other* people.

There are times, many times really, when our true and former selves begin to elude us, like dog hair from a broom. We are no longer people; we are parents. Our illusions of grandeur turn into delusions of being able to watch a ballgame, in perfect peace, for three consecutive plays. I realize that women – my wife included, to be sure — bear much of this burden, and that their identities are often snuffed out by the suffocating demands of motherhood. But in guiding kids through the maze of youth, anybody, even a dad, can get lost.

This business of parenthood, this all-consuming task of steadying wobbly squirts into upstanding citizens, goes largely against my genetic grain. I am in many ways a loner. A loner with social tendencies, sure, and not of the Unabomber genus, but a loner nevertheless. Many people who put pen to paper are prone to moodiness and retreat. When you live with literary voices in your head, there is sometimes no room for the literal world. It is nothing personal or intentional; we tick the way we tick.

At times I'm able to transform this soundtrack of all-things-children into a kind of otherworldly white noise. I hear nothing, and the world is still. Other times, I am just a bouncing ball in a game of Pong, circa 1977, set to the music of Donna Summer. Back and forth I go, up and down, volleying to and fro, seemingly never accomplishing much of anything. My patience runs thin, my frustration high. I don't read (polysyllabic) books. I don't listen to (adult) music. I no longer speak in complete sentences or use big-boy words. I hear everything but myself.

Naturally, in the spirit of O. Henry, I am a kid magnet. I once spent seven consecutive months with my son dragging on my leg, causing me both mental and bodily duress (this is hyperbole; it was five). I am usually the designated kid thrower in the pool and often the proverbial dog-and-pony show at birthday parties. When I want to hide, kids seek me. I am a proton; they are electrons buzzing about. I'll admit that this is sometimes my own fault. Children, after all, are an easy mark when it comes to humor, and their howls aren't fabricated or forced. To them, the light to the laugh track is always on.

I am fortunate in that my children let me follow my own dreams, provided my own dreams occur between their bedtime and dawn's first light. And since they are in such similar stages of life – ages 10, 4 and 3 months – getting them to bed is peaceful and seamless. This is sarcasm.

Now, the bottom line. It is accurate that I am often out of my comfort zone. Yes, there are times that I want to take a family vacation that doesn't include any human taller than 48 inches. This is, I hope, completely normal, especially when normal is so often a distant oasis. Still, I wouldn't trade any of it, or them, for a minute (well, maybe for a minute, or two days). Not my son's bear hugs or my daughter's lounge-club act or my baby's squeaky snores. Not the (now) five of us bumbling and battling and braving life together. None of it. Fatherhood may very well not be entrenched in my DNA, but that doesn't mean that the kids don't get my TLC. Sure, I sometimes happily put my son on the school bus, but don't think that I wouldn't readily jump in front of it in his defense. No matter where I turn, I can't seem to shake my kids, which is okay because, like it or not, they'll never be able to shake me.

I think most any parent can relate. We can be nauseating, to be sure, to those who don't have children. We are nauseated, on occasion, by our own. We are tired and frustrated and usually more Clark Kent than SuperParent. We fall short of expectations and demands and time. We wrestle with our imperfections and get pinned down by guilt. We try hard to recall more carefree, simple times, but we cannot. But we get back up, pulled by obligation and affection and the fact that we can't legally hock them on Craig's List. We cut the Bit O' Honey out of the boy's hair and flick the gunk out of the baby's eyes and, because the girl has to be at gymnastics practice in 11 minutes, we carry on. We tear out and merge, with The Wiggles wiggling on the DVD player, back into strife in the fast lane.

Our hopes can be only that we were provided a solid parenting blueprint by our own parents, which Jennifer and I both were, and that luck and genetics and labor fall into place to produce decent and law-abiding adults. And that one day, once we are pardoned for good behavior, one of our kids, ideally the one that was the biggest pain in the butt, will take us to Luby's on his dime.

(Disclaimer: The above was a gross generalization of kids and parents. I certainly was not referring to any child who was sitting quietly and obediently doing TAKS workbooks just for kicks while you peacefully read the above.)

Three kids. No wife. Rain. Cold. No babysitter. This weekend oughta fly by.

The true meaning behind and sweet beauty of kids' birthday parties comes not from the shiny presents or budding friendships but instead in having someplace to dump your brat for two hours.

The backseat of my car looks like a fast-food joint, complete with wrappers, renegade fries and some wide-eyed cashier named Zed.

Kids today have no excuse to not be smarter than their parents. They have the Internet and entire channels angled toward education. We had our folks' encyclopedias, a few lame shows on PBS and Scooby Doo chasing clues (with special animated guest stars Don Knotts and Tim Conway!).

Manning the fort solo this weekend. Sharpening the Benadryl darts and digging the McDonald's straws out of the trash.

If you ever feel the need to feel needed, have a kid or three.

Dear Pixar: Thank you, thank you, thank you. I love you so very, very much.

With all due respect to The Battle of the Bulge and The Battle of Iwo Jima, I'm more concerned with The Battle of Bathtime, The Battle of Bedtime and The Battle of Hey-Kids-Stop-Locking-Us-Outta-The-Master-Bathroom.

Why do some parents have such a hard time entertaining their kids on the weekends? It's easy around here — one rakes, the other bags.

Kids don't play outdoors anymore. Instead, they surf the Internet because it's too hot outside. On both counts, I blame Al Gore.

With flashbacks to Mr. Duzan's searing paddle, I invariably and obediently walk on the green stripe when taking the kids to school, silently with eyes straight ahead.

Lot of young chunks at the neighborhood pool yesterday, raising both my concern for their future health and the water level.

Thought Stretch was pretty hard on Pat this morning on Handy Manny by calling him a "great big tool."

Excited for the kids and the beginning of their summers. The girl looks cute in a hard hat, while the boy is handy with a shoe horn.

If protractors were still included on kids' back-to-school supply lists, parents would form spirited protest rallies and call for the abolishment of all things pointy.

Flying with the kids. Trying to decide which one will get the oxygen mask first if there is an emergency. Have opted to pick the one with the most earning potential.

Kids have elixirs for every malady these days; when we were little, our moms either gobbed Vicks or sprayed Bactine on it.

My kids most certainly wouldn't beat up your honor student; however, I wouldn't be a bit surprised if they cheated off your kid's paper.

Have gone two rounds with Barney, with a third likely to come. I try to tell the kids not to place too much stock in a dinosaur who sings "Macaroni, macaroni, mac and cheese. Three times daily, pretty please!?" Three times daily? That's excessive.

I have serious doubts that kids today would know the proper technique involved in drinking from a neighbor's garden hose.

By the time our kids are teens, we'll have the technology to know their whereabouts at practically all times; this fact both comforts and scares the crap out of me.

These kids of mine climb on me so much that I'm legally changing my name to Gym.

I honestly think Physics should be introduced in kindergarten. Kids take a beating before ever learning squat about the Law of Gravity.

They're everywhere, these three kids. There's Mudd all over the floor. I'm beginning to think the only logical solution is to move to a polygamist state.

Pop Culture

I can't tell you very much about the war in the Middle East.

But I can tell you too much about the battlefield that is Paris Hilton's heart.

I can't remember where I left my car keys.

But I can remember the point in which Mr. Brady went from straight locks to the man perm (season five).

I don't know the names of the cabinet members.

But I know every cast member's name from the sitcom "Growing Pains."

I can't report on topics that most people consider essential to everyday life.

But I can report that rocker Eddie Money was once a New York City policeman.

Such is the minimum-security prison that is my brain, and I'm 42 years into a life sentence. Despite making (mostly) good grades and earning a (modest-paying profession) degree from a (somewhat reputable) college, this passion for pop culture minutia and music (and sports) trivia teasers has always left more of a (skid) mark on my brain. My thoughts have just never seemed to go with the flow. Even now, writing that, I miss Flo, the sassy, gum-smacking waitress from the underrated sitcom "Alice."

We all have a junk drawer at home; I have one between my ears.

To wit:

Negotiations over relations with my wife remind me of movie lines ("It's hovering over its primary target and preparing its probing device!" – Independence Day).

There is nobody in my life that I can't instantly compare to a song (My jargon-spewing doctor, for instance, "Blinds Me with Science.").

Ritz crackers remind me of tacos ("Putting on the Ritz," by, of course, Taco).

Most everybody knows that Hank Aaron broke Babe Ruth's home run record, but I'm saddled with the useless baggage of knowing who threw the pitch (Al Downing) and who the catcher (Joe Ferguson), leftfielder (Bill Buckner) and announcer (Curt Gowdy) were. Oh, and that relief pitcher Tom House chased down the ball in the bullpen after prying it away from a lupus-stricken child named Timmy.

(Okay, I made Timmy up for dramatic effect).

If you need help doing an Excel spreadsheet or fixing the leaky sink, though, you're out of luck.

I'll admit it's something of a crutch when one's brain misfires on most cylinders, but there are some perks for knowing stuff not worth knowing. For instance, I realized early on that the mastery of math was not for me; however, if I could use sports trivia smarts to later dial up the digits of a young maiden, well, that was just a solid appropriation of available brain funds.

For instance:

Scene: Some bar. 1:49 a.m. 1991.

Me: So, what's your number?

She: 316-6885.

Pause.

Me: Okay, got it.

She: You're not even going to write it down? You'll never remember it.

(Note: Those were the days when we punched phone numbers into soggy napkins, not contact lists.)

Me: Of course I will. 3. Babe Ruth. 16. Joe Montana. 6. Dr. J. 88. Drew Pearson. 5. Johnny Bench. Easy wheezy.

Girl walks away mumbling something.

(Note: I believe this to be an actual phone number that I remember. But don't call her. It was 20 years ago, plus she wasn't that great-looking. It was 1:49 a.m.)

I wish I had an alibi, that I was "with a friend" when my "sense of practical thinking" was hijacked, but I really don't. I am left-handed. I flip through magazines from back to front. My favorite number is 13. I am a Virgo, so, along with crying often (even now, tears are streaming down my face) and being a lousy driver, I am susceptible to strangeness. Every secret password I've ever owned includes the jersey number of my favorite player from the 1980 Cleveland Browns. I am even-keeled on the surface but internally, eternally a little odd.

I can't imagine that we are a very proud bunch, those of us who can barely remember the way home but can recite the choice lines of every John Hughes movie. Nor are we the best and the brightest. We wish we grasped the real nuts and bolts of life, the stuff our dads (tried to) teach us. The stuff you talk about on conference calls and what you consultants consult about. We really do. We just don't think that stuff is very fun.

We hoarders of the irrelevant, however, are handy for bar bets and make nice party favors. After all, I don't *really* care what you do for a living, but, say, can you name the four major universities whose mascots don't end with the letter 's'? (Trivia note: those mascots with a color – Crimson Tide, Blue Devils, for example don't count.)

I can.

In retrospect, except for John Davidson's hair, much of what was featured on the 80's variety TV show "That's Incredible!" really wasn't all that incredible.

Glad he's fish food, but curious why it took so long when Osama spent five years in a house that all but featured a neon sign shouting Bin Lad Inn.

Even pitchman Sam Elliot's voice sounds like it needs a shower.

Carlos Silva, a mediocre pitcher for the Chicago Cubs, is released and paid $11.5 million for his time; meanwhile, 350 Round Rock ISD teachers are fired for free. The moral is that life, in instances too many to count, blows.

Anybody born between 1965-70 need not feel guilty about not ending up cool. Our role model for coolness was Henry Winkler.

"You need the light and the dark." I tend to believe that, especially when spoken by noted philosopher Jennifer Aniston.

The vocal chords of Morgan Freeman just earned more narrating those three movie trailers than my entire body will earn all year.

Twitter gives us 140 characters to share our thoughts. That's plenty. Some people don't have nearly that much character.

Never get too complacent – Nick Nolte was once voted People Magazine's Sexiest Man Alive, and Bruce Jenner was once crowned the World's Greatest Athlete.

Saw that Tony Danza is getting yet another show, breaking the number of chances previously held by a cat.

The Y-M-C-A is officially changing its name to the Y, forcing the Police Officer, the Chief and the Construction Worker into early retirement.

Oft-injured Bret Michaels should have known that years of playing with Poison would eventually catch up with him.

Bill Gates lives in a 50,050-square foot home. Because he needed that 50 extra square feet for incidentals.

I was once a card-carrying member of the KISS Army, but because of my reluctance to wear makeup before my tenth birthday, I never advanced beyond the rank of private.

Cooking beef stroganoff over the medium-high heat of Charlie Sheen's fire-breathing fists.

One day we will all reside in a municipality called Amazooglebucks, where a barista will whisk your latte and answer your nagging question about the life expectancy of an aardvark while express ordering you window treatments and Grisham's latest.

I love the movie "Training Day." Brings back childhood memories, likely a result from growing up on such a tough cul-de-sac.

Think it was God's plan to miss work yesterday, if only to catch up on Bo and Hope's storyline after a 22-year hiatus.

I was set to jump at the chance to purchase an entire 80's hair band for $1.29 at Taco Bell, then realized the marquee was promoting 5layer, not Slayer, burritos.

Most every famous writer whose mug is featured on this Kindle default screen looks like the former Chastity Bono.

When I was nine, I won a season's pass to Water Wonderland by proving to a kid that the guy was singing about "Feelings," not "Felix."

Back to once prove that you're never too old to be a rock star or too odd-looking to marry a supermodel, The Cars have a new song.

I don't want to see the "untrimmed chest" of Train's lead singer any more than he wants to check out "My Sharona."

Saw an ad for new Trojan "Fire" condoms – because the wife and I are looking for that burning sensation during relations.

Without so much as the escort of a white Ford Bronco, I was just forced to sprint through the airport.

Not too proud to admit that I like to keep up with the Kardashians. In fact, I like to think that they expect and depend on it.

The Broadway musical "Cats" ran for 19 straight years. Reason for finally closing – really, really tired.

Not ashamed to admit that I learned how to approach women, fearlessly and leading with the lips, from Richard Dawson of "Family Feud."

I was once cussed out by Potsy Webber at the Odessa Holidome. It was funny as a crutch.

As the years pass, I find myself fantasizing that a contestant on "The Wheel of Fortune" will spin the wheel backwards, causing Vanna White to de-age like Benjamin Button.

I've seen Elton John and Billy Joel in concert together. Amazing show, especially with the dueling pianos. Even better, though, would be a hot dog eating contest between the two.

Woke to a headline that read "Bad News for Bacon, Hot Dog Lovers." Didn't read on – my love is unconditional.

Can't help but think that if Smart Water *really* worked, then product spokesperson Jennifer Aniston would be making better movie choices by now.

Kindly old lady told me that I look like actor John Cusack. I said, "Oh yeah? You oughta see me in a trenchcoat." Kindly old lady caned away.

Gays and lesbians understandably pay tribute to those like Ellen DeGeneres and the fella from N'Sync. However, I feel like one brave soul has been forgotten by history – Peppermint Patty.

Yesterday, Prince William turned Katherine into a princess; over the coming years, there will inevitably be times when he'll think of her as simply a royal pain.

Ryan Seacrest is everywhere. He's Casey Kasem. He's our Tom Brokaw. The guy is a human spork.

The first '45' I ever bought was "Reunited" by Peaches & Herbs. There, I said it. (And it felt so good.)

Sure, landing a fighter jet on an aircraft carrier or disarming a bomb are both harrowing, white-knuckle moments, but neither measure up to the sheer pressure of standing at a Redbox video hut with four people waiting behind you in line.

I learned most everything I know about politics from Schoolhouse Rock.

When you listen to the song "Sister Christian," much of it is kind of nonsensical, but I still love her, and I always will.

Godspeed, Sherwood Schwartz, creator of "The Brady Bunch" and others. Thank you for letting me ride you through my adolescence. That didn't sound right.

Cooking some chicken pot pies for the family. We'll eat in 14 hours, when they cool down a bit.

Have read that when you have sex with someone, you're allegedly having sex with the last seven people they've been with. If this is true, I would imagine that by now we've all nailed either Pam Anderson or Kid Rock.

You were either a Mister Rogers guy or a Captain Kangaroo guy. You couldn't be both.

Farrah Fawcett starred on "Charlie's Angels" for just one season, but she hung on my wall for at least five and in my thoughts for much longer.

Walked past a group watching "The Bachelor." If you listened closely, you could actually hear their collective IQs dropping.

My understanding of computers has never advanced much beyond the movie "War Games."

Never been a huge Aaron Neville fan, even less so after I learned that even his mole has groupies.

Went to the Journey concert last night. The lead singer does a better Steve Perry than Steve Perry but could not beat Prince in a jump ball.

Have an Iphone and an Ipod and Itunes. What I really need, though, are Iglasses.

Facebook makes high school reunions obsolete. I already know what you're doing, where you've been, the names of your kids and that you ate stuffed bell peppers last night.

At our house, we're trying to bring back the "gimme five." No knuckles, no hand jives. Just gimme five.

Global warming, eh. It doesn't seem *that* much hotter than it was when I was a kid. What *is* markedly hotter? Female softball players.

James Franco seemed demure and professional last night in hosting the Oscars. And by demure and professional I mean profoundly paranoid and incredibly high.

Have always questioned the ferocity of Alanis Morrisette's "You Oughta Know" after factoring in that it was written about zany Uncle Joey of "Full House."

Big fan of all things Paul Rudd; he's like a fun-sized Chris Farley.

I've considered auditioning for "Survivor" and think I would have at least an outside chance of making it. What stops me is the knowledge that potentially going weeks without manscaping would render me virtually unrecognizable.

Every single sex-education film that I can remember watching included a van, a hip cat named Chuck and a really loud-talking narrator saying: "And *always* stay out of the back of a van, or you're highly likely to catch the gonorrhea."

Thx 2 txtng, good spelling is sewww 2008.

If (random character actor) Robert Loggia blew into my kitchen at 7 a.m. pimping Sunny Delight, I'd be inclined to blow him away.

One of the greatest acts of human bravery, other than defending our country or sitting through an entire Rob Schneider movie, is trying to successfully infiltrate a circle of dancing women.

This first-edition Ipod of mine holds the power of the Texas governor.

Eating Lemonheads candy reminds me of watching "The Bad News Bears in Breaking Training" for the 17th time at the Scott Theater, which makes me feel nine again, which makes me happy.

At the cinema watching "How to Train Your Dragon." With this suave evolution of 3D glasses, it feels like I'm sitting alongside a bunch of Joels from Risky Business.

Brett Favre has trusted the affordable quality of Wrangler jeans his entire life. No he hasn't. Yes he has. Well, maybe he has.

Tough day for pitcher Roger Clemens: (1) Indicted on federal perjury charges and (2) scheduled to play in a celebrity pro-am golf tourney with his wife.

Despite the herd of Austin bumper stickers trumpeting optimism and rebirth and change, I just had an iffy feeling about President Obama when I found out he bowled a 37 on the campaign trail.

Love & Marriage

I can still see her, even now, 25 years later.

When I was about 17, I developed a crystal-clear image of the Perfect Woman. She had blue eyes and long, blonde hair pulled back in a ponytail and tucked under a baseball cap. She wore a jean skirt and beat-up cowboy boots on her tan legs and drove a red Jeep. Together, we would take drives along the river until we parked under a tree and drank Lone Star beer while listening to Johnny Cougar (c'mon, it was 1985).

In real life, this Perfect Woman would have never looked my way. But it was my dream, and my dream insisted that she only had eyes for me.

If one were to put a Love Detector to my heart, it would probably tell you that, although it's skipped a beat on many occasions, only four times has it been hooked. With the first one, the high school sweetheart, I suppose I didn't yet know what love was, not really. I wasn't quite ready to love the college crush, and love, as it does when left untended, faded away. As for Bachelorette #3, I never could figure out, despite my best efforts, how to correctly love her. As I neared my thirties, my feet and I seemed firmly implanted in bachelorhood, and I thought I'd either end up a priest or a pimp.

To say that I swept Jennifer off her feet would be a bit dramatic, a little too Fabio. We worked at the same newspaper and stole glances at each other. Her brother and I were friends. We were both in relationships, and when they ran their course, I asked her out for dinner and a movie. She was pretty and fun and laughed at my jokes. She had a kind heart and smiling eyes and, best of all, was a NASP (normal-acting stable person). She was, and still is, a keeper.

Together we've been ever since.

I wish I could blow your hair back with adventurous tales of my chivalry or boast about the long-distance dedication I once sent her way via Casey Kasem (during which I penned a handwritten six-page letter and requested that Casey play "I Only Wanna Be with You," by Hootie & the Blowfish). I cannot. We admired each other, then we liked each other, then we loved each other. It was the way things work in the unscripted world, where officers don't carry textile workers away as the closing credits roll. Our courtship was tidy and sweet and followed the natural order of the cosmos.

There is often little natural about marriage or parenthood or essentially turning (five) moving pieces into one working part. Things sometimes fall off track, and the wheels of marital momentum skid to a halt. Days turn to nights and into the next day, and we ease into the oft- unspoken domestic dance of working and parenting and simply surviving. We speak in starts and stops but don't have time for the specifics. Conversations turn into quick exchanges, often broken by off-stage demands (Mom! Juice! *Geez!*). Romance gets squashed under the weight of the day, and passion becomes something that you pencil in for a week from Sunday at 10:24p. What you feel you're left with, as the days and years blur by, is a runaway train called marriage and family.

My wife keeps us all on course and in check. Our brood, the shopping, the bills, work, me, pretty much the whole enchilada (even, ironically, the enchiladas). She juggles duties as John Mayer does women. I may wake with a couple of tasks to tackle. I don't bother to write these down because, well, it's not too much to remember. Jennifer enters a day with three dozen or so directives, most of which she writes down on Post-It notes scattered about because, well, it's far too much to remember. My wife – and perhaps wives and mothers and women in general – seems to be equipped with an internal Marks-A-Lot that, the day's hurdles be damned, allows her to pick off chores in militant fashion. (We men, yeah, we don't really have that. Give us food, give us sleep, give us sex, and we're pretty good.) In these respects, my wife is a dead-eye sniper of all things domestic. We would be lost without her; she is our compass, our GPS.

(Note: To be fair, I'm not exactly a slug around our shack. While no Alice of "The Brady Bunch," I can handle a Swiffer and can locate the laundry room and have even been known, on occasion, to concoct something edible. In raising kids while working, one must often assume an androgynous stance. Anyway, let the record show...)

I do have a confession to make, as long as it stays between you and me. We are not the Perfect Couple. I know it sounds crazy, but it's true. I put the blame squarely on the fact that we are, in fact, two humans wrestling under the same air space. It is a delicate balance, the merging of one life to another, especially when one of the lives belongs to me (See: Loner, I am a), and we fall prey, like any Jack and Jill, to the traps. We are forced to divide and conquer, then we forget to reconvene at headquarters. We (silently) keep score in regards to the division of labor, that who-does-more game in which there are no real winners. Sometimes I pull as she pushes; sometimes she yings when I yang. Worst of all, we let the largeness of life overshadow the smallness of us. And, sure, we have battles – or squirmishes, as CNN would report – but we rarely wage war. We save those for the kids, and I'm hopeful we still have ammo left once they hit puberty.

Listen, you can't take that sweet little ditty read at most every wedding as the everyday gospel. Love isn't *always* patient or kind. It can, in fact, be bitter and, certainly, it can brood. We are not *always* best friends. This is not meant to be sad or pessimistic. Only honest and pragmatic. This is the real world – marriage – not Disney World.

Truth be told, I've only known one Perfect Couple. They were sweet and clingy and blonde and nauseating. They sent out Christmas "year in review" letters and played co-ed flag football together. And behind their white picket fence, as it turned out, they hated each other.

We lean, I believe, on the same little victories and simple pleasures that any (still) married couple does. Sharing inside jokes. Giving each other some good-natured ribbing. Laughing about times gone by. Holding hands in the movies. Having each other's back. Finding company in misery. Doing little things that often mean a lot. Affording each other distance while remaining close. Watching our family grow. Watching our life unfold. Together.

And loving, in spite of it all, and because of it all, without leaving.

I intended to make this section more of a general commentary on women. I am, after all, surrounded by them almost every day. I have been exposed to more estrogen than the proverbial gay friend. But let's be real. If I were to take a swipe at encapsulating the female species – if most *any* man were to attempt to solve that riddle – then that passage would promptly be stripped of its many inaccuracies, struck of its foolish assumptions and whittled down to a single sentence.

Generally speaking, we know nothing.

So all I can do is learn as much as I can, day to day, year by year, about the most important one in my life. I know that she loves South Congress Cafe and hates pickles and is indifferent to politics. I know she is a loyal friend and that she loves to dance and that she sends out handwritten thank-you notes without exception. I know her favorite movies hail from the 80's and that she would consider leaving me for Matt Damon and that she likes the house temperature to rival that of

Antarctica (even now, a penguin is shivering at my feet). I know she loves to jog and to laugh but sometimes feels like running and crying. These details are important because they are the stuff that a husband simply must know.

I also know she loves her kids and her family, fiercely so. And that she loves her job. And that, in good times and bad, she loves me. And I know that it's hard for her, being a mom, being a teacher, being a wife, being everything to everyone, all of the time. I get it, even when it seems like I don't. And I want her to know that I love and admire her for it.

(And in case I never properly said it: Thank you three times over, Jennifer, for carrying our kids. That must have been really uncomfortable.)

So we are not always perfect. But maybe we are perfect for each other, Jennifer and I. Our success is slow and measured and sure. We are today and tomorrow and the day after that. We are for better and for worse and for the many muddled times in between. And we are, like a side-view mirror, much closer than we might sometimes appear.

Besides, we have three kids. Who else would want us?

I like to imagine that my Perfect Woman of 1985 is today twice divorced and lives in a trailer just outside of Sacramento, where her rusty Jeep sits on blocks. She could really use a fitness trainer, and her legs are no longer tanned. How could they be? She spends all day inside at the Wal-Mart, where she works double shifts and can't find a damn Johnny Cougar cassette tape anywhere.

It was my dream, after all, and I say her life went into the shitter without me.

Married my wife a few hours before soccer player Brandi Chastain ripped off her jersey. That day, we both scored.

Wishing a happy birthday to my {insert glowing adjective here} wife, who puts up with me even when I'm {insert not-so-glowing adjective here}.

The wife just surprised me with a trip to Las Vegas for my 40th birthday. She packed extra clothes and everything, which is good, because I think I just crapped my pants.

The wife and I, in anticipation of the new no-texting-and-driving law, have been having reckless, gratuitous, epic car text.

When a man and a woman lock eyes for the first time, the woman may smile but will invariably look away and never look back. The man, if given the chance and provisions, would try to regain eye contact for 5-7 years.

My late-and-great Pop's secret to marriage: "Your mother makes all the small decisions, and I make all the big ones. In 50-plus years of marriage, we still haven't had a big decision to make." Classic.

It's me and the boy here at home surrounded by chicks — Jennifer, McKenzie, Ellen, Oprah, Kelly, Chelsea...

The wife and I are returning from a private paradise in Mexico, where we sunned and napped and played and had more (language) misunderstandings than an episode of "Three's Company."

Tough being the husband of a drill team director; the wife has more events than a decathlete.

I'm all for women getting their little black dresses, just as long as we can have our big set of golf clubs.

There are certain times in every husband's life when he has to stand up for what he believes to be right and honest and fair. This isn't one of those times.

I understand women on about the same level as I do the Renaissance Fair.

Here at the county courthouse. My wife and I get bossed around by our kids so much that we've decided to legally our names to Tony Micelli and Angela Bauer.

My Cleveland Indians are batting .145 as a team this month. Shoot, even I score more than that.

With my family out of town, I plan to have some Chinese food, the same cuisine that the wife pretended to enjoy, along with golf and sports and camping, while we were dating.

(Another) Rapture coming tomorrow.
Men will gather provisions; women will scramble to find out what everyone else is going to wear.

The wife is really hot and bothered tonight; the A/C just went out.

When someone, particularly someone of the opposite sex, ends a sentence with "annyyywayyy" at a party, you are effectively dismissed from that conversation.

Like many couples, the wife and I have a figurative "free pass" person. I told her that mine was Eva Longoria; she countered with Billy the Firefighter from three doors down.

The only thing more interesting than sitting in a park and eavesdropping on new mothers talk about the eating and sleeping and bowel habits of their children is, well, nothing is more interesting than that.

The wife and I made a united stand against the kids; today, neither one of us can stand them.

Not a huge fan of when women do their nails in that extra-long, blocked-off style. What is that? I can only assume it's for digging holes and burying money.

The wife and I sometimes struggle with the whole division of labor thing…we both stink in math.

I like to think of myself as a trophy husband. Sure, I'm a bowling trophy, but still.

Not sure why all the fuss about these mandatory power outages; any husband, if honest, will tell you that they rarely have power at home.

A good husband knows not to tell his wife absolutely everything about his past; this isn't Taxi Cab Confessions.

For men unhappy in their own relationships, consider the Green Spoon Worm, which is 200,000 times smaller than its female mate and spends its entire two-month lifespan in her sexual tract, regurgitating sperm in an effort to impregnate her several times over before dying.

The mutual passion that the wife and I share, the common thread that holds our bond together, the unspoken force that guides us, is our shared love of burned potato chips.

Sharks can smell blood from a quarter-mile away. Impressive, until you consider that my wife can smell a shoe sale from three counties over.

Recent study shows that women, on average, smile 62 times a day, compared to just 8 for men. This leads me to believe that the women used in the study were reading this book.

Made in the USA
Lexington, KY
23 August 2011